I0139618

THE TABERNACLE

A REVELATION OF JESUS CHRIST

Dr. Gregory Pittman Sr.

The Tabernacle a Revelation of Jesus Christ

© Copyright 2002
© Copyright 2024 Revised
Dr. Gregory Pittman Sr.

Printed in the United States of America
All rights reserved. No part of this book can be reproduced in any form without the express written permission from the author, except in the case of brief quotations, critical articles or reviews.

GPS PUBLISHING L.L.C.
1315 Oakfield Dr. Ste. 2914
Brandon, FL 33509
gpspublishing2662@gmail.com

All scripture unless otherwise noted are from the King James Version of the Bible.

ISBN 979-8-9899177-0-9

Table of Contents

The Tabernacle a Revelation of Jesus Christ

Table of Contents

The Tabernacle a Revelation of Jesus Christ

Dedication

I want to dedicate this book to the first woman I ever loved and the first to ever love me. I called her mom, and she called me son. As I grew in the grace of God she became my friend who I shared my thoughts and dreams, and she listened to them all, and always encouraged me with these words: "You can do anything you set your mind to!"

Therefore, Evangelist Dr. Fannie A. Pittman, I trusted in your words because I saw the Living God guiding your life and knew He would guide mine wheresoever the sole of my foot should tread. Thank you mother for always living a godly life before us.

The Tabernacle a Revelation of Jesus Christ

Introduction

"But these are written, that ye might believe that Jesus is the Christ, the Son of God; and that believing ye might have life through His name" (John 20:31). We are admonished by Christ to "Search the scriptures; for in them ye think ye have eternal life: and they are they which testify of me" (John 5:39).

The entire Bible contains within Its pages keys of life. And within those pages are keys of revelation. This word "revelation" is from the Greek; *"Apokolupis"* which means an *"unveiling"* our bible is a revelation or an unveiling of the Almighty God, His plans and purposes for mankind. In it we see creation from its beginning; we see sin entering into that perfect creation and marring its beauty, its innocence and its potential. But there we also see, the merciful, loving God, preparing the way to rectify what man had done

The Tabernacle a Revelation of Jesus Christ

(through disobedience) to His creative work, through the redemptive work of His Son Jesus Christ. And through this sovereign act of redemption, we can once again come into perfect fellowship with God. And it is through the Holy Scriptures, that God has chosen to reveal the glory of His Son.

As we walk through the Bible we are not long in waiting to see the Tabernacle, God's revealing hand, unveiling that shadow of that which is to come.

The Tabernacle is a divine revelation of Jesus Christ. And as has been stated already, a revelation is an *"unveiling"* of some hidden truths. The Tabernacle is just that; it is an unveiling, a revelation of Jesus Christ.

The Tabernacle a Revelation of Jesus Christ

Every aspect as you will see speaks of, and points to our redeemer, Jesus Christ. God always intended for man to know Him, and He reveals Himself through His Only Begotten Son Jesus Christ. In the Tabernacle He reveals these truths; and anyone who wants to know Him must study the Tabernacle and its types to obtain a deeper knowledge of Christ.

For I have been spiritually blessed, renewed and strengthened through the research on this subject. I thank God for His guidance and revelation, and to the authors from whom I have drawn heavily. I am grateful for the invaluable assistance received from the following authors in writing this book: Kevin J. Conner, The Tabernacle of Moses, Theodore H. Epp, Portraits of Christ in the Tabernacle, Ada R. Habershon Outline studies of the Tabernacle, and a number of other books several of which are listed in the bibliography of this book.

I am grateful to God for all the teachers, preachers, and people He has allowed to impart invaluable, knowledge and understanding. The most honor belongs to God who has added some wisdom to mingle with, and to enhance the understanding. All praise be unto God Almighty for the work of His Son Jesus Christ.

Chapter 1

The Divine Purpose of the Tabernacle

The Divine purpose of the Tabernacle may be summed up in the verses found in Exodus 25:8; and 29:45-46; "Let them make me a sanctuary that I may dwell among them."

It was God's desire to dwell in the midst of His people. Man was created for the great purpose of having fellowship with God. Epp states: that God had three distinct purposes in mind for the Tabernacle: "God planned to dwell in the midst of Israel; to teach man the Holiness of God and the sinfulness of mankind; and to show sinful man the only way to salvation."[1]

We can, after knowing more about God, wholeheartedly agree with Epp, to the plurality of God's purpose, but, for the novice who only knows God in a limited way or, for the outsider desiring to

---

[1] Theodore H. Epp, <u>Portraits of Christ in the Tabernacle</u> pg.45

draw close, and even the skeptic, the Divine purpose of the Tabernacle is God's desire to dwell with mankind.

Our word "tabernacle" is derived from the Hebrew word. *Mishkan,* which means, *A residence, a dwelling place or habitation.*[2] And from its root word: *Shaken* which means to *abide or continue to dwel*l. And He still desires to dwell among His people, which Christ fulfilled when He was the "Word made flesh and dwelt among us" (John 1:14). And He will ultimately dwell among the redeemed: "And I heard a great voice out of heaven saying, Behold, the tabernacle of God is with men, and He will dwell with them, and they shall be His people, and God Himself shall be with them, and be their God." (Revelation 21:3).

---

[2] James Strong, <u>The New Exhaustive Concordance of the Bible</u> pg. 1031

The Tabernacle a Revelation of Jesus Christ

The requirements for the construction of the Tabernacle

"According to all that I shew thee, after the pattern of the tabernacle, and the pattern of all the instruments thereof, even so shall ye make it." (Exodus25:9).

Fifteen times in Exodus chapters 39-40, we hear the phrase *"As the LORD commanded Moses"* and three times we hear, According *"to all that the LORD commanded Moses."* The emphasis on the construction of the tabernacle is that it had to be specifically made according to a Divine pattern.

There could be no deviation from what was obviously revealed to Moses by God. Epp states: "Any deviation from God's pattern in the tabernacle would bring a curse on Israel."[3]

According to Conner: The Sevenfold requirements for the building of the Tabernacle were:

---

[3] Theodore H. Epp Portraits of Christ in the Tabernacle pg.41

The Tabernacle a Revelation of Jesus Christ

• By free will offering, "Speak unto the children of Israel, that they bring me an offering: of every man that giveth it willingly with his heart

ye shall take my offering." (Exodus 25:2).

• By a people stirred up "And they came, every one whose heart stirred him up" (35:21).

• "every one whose heart stirred him up to come unto the work to do it" (Exodus 36:2).

• By a people made willing "Everyone whom his spirit made willing." (Exodus 25:21). God's people are to be willing to do His will.

• By a free-hearted people. The people gave these offerings freely as a heart response to the goodness of the Lord. "And they brought yet unto him free offerings every morning." (Exodus 36:3).

• By the wisdom of God "and every wise hearted man, in whom the LORD put wisdom and understanding to know how to work all manner of work for the service of the sanctuary, according to all that the LORD had commanded." (Exodus 36:1). The Tabernacle was built by the wisdom of God through Moses.

The Tabernacle a Revelation of Jesus Christ

• By the Spirit of God "And he hath filled him with the spirit of God, in wisdom, in understanding, and in knowledge, and in all manner of workmanship." (Exodus 35:31).

The Tabernacle was by enabling and equipping of the Holy Spirit upon men. The New Testament Church can only be built accordingly (Zechariah 4:6).

According to the Divine pattern: "Moses was admonished of God when he was about to make the tabernacle: for, See, saith he, *that* thou make all things according to the pattern shewed to thee in the mount." (Hebrews 8:5). Nothing was left to the mind or imagination of man. Everything was made according to God's pattern. God can only bless and seal with glory that which is done according to the standard of His word. The New Testament Church will also have to measure up to the pattern of God.[4]

The Tabernacle was the place where God came to meet man, and it represented the one in whom Deity

---

[4] Kevin J. Conner The Tabernacle of Mosespg.9-10

The Tabernacle a Revelation of Jesus Christ

and humanity met-the Lord Jesus Christ. Every feature of the Tabernacle prefigured the Person and work of Christ.[5]

The entire Tabernacle and its components, services and sacrifices were a type of the perfect Christ. As there are no imperfections in Christ, ("And of His fullness have we all received" John 1:16a) there could be none in the Tabernacle. All was done "As the LORD commanded Moses," nothing was left to human ingenuity. God saw every detail, the people were not even permitted to give in any fashion, they had to give God's way, by a freewill offering. No other mind could have devised such a glorious structure with such endless amounts of knowledge within itself except the Creator God Himself. It would be Impossible for human wisdom to even begin to contemplate such a structure, because anything that man does is tainted by sin and therefore, cannot be accepted by God, except it be done according to the pattern, which is: "Not by might, nor by power, but by my spirit, saith the LORD of hosts." (Zechariah 4:6).

---

[5] Theodore H. Epp <u>Portraits of Christ in the Tabernacle</u> pg.15

The Tabernacle a Revelation of Jesus Christ

Location of the Tabernacle

"And the LORD spake unto Moses and unto Aaron, saying, Every man of the children of Israel shall pitch by his own standard, with the ensign of their father's house: far off about the tabernacle of the congregation shall they pitch." (Numbers 2:1-2).

The tabernacle was situated in the center of the camp surrounded by the twelve tribes, which revealed that God was dwelling in the midst of His people not just among them. It was a type of the "Word made flesh, that dwelt among us" (John 1:14), in the Person of Jesus Christ. It is also a type of Christ in the midst of the church (Rev. 1:13; 2:1). It provided easy access to God, and also protection from the enemy.

On the East: Judah, Issachar and Zebulon these totaled 186,000 individuals and they were under the standard of the Lion.

On the west: Ephraim, Manasseh, and Benjamin these totaled 108,000 individuals and they were under the standard of the Ox.

The Tabernacle a Revelation of Jesus Christ

The Tabernacle a Revelation of Jesus Christ

On the north: Dan, Asher and Naphtali, who totaled 157,000 individuals, and camped under the standard of the Eagle.

On the south: Gad Ruben and Simeon these totaled 151,450 individuals who camped under the standard of the Man.

Conner states: "Therefore with all the tribes in their place we have a very interesting picture, not in man's view, but in God's. For with all the tribes so arranged on the North, South, East and West with the Tabernacle in the midst from a heavenly view we would see the camp arranged in the shape of a cross…This is Divine Order!'[6]

Names given to the Tabernacle

Some of the names given to the Tabernacle are:

The Tabernacle of the Congregation which was to be the place where the people gathered together at the door. Epp says: "It is of the congregation," which reveals there was only one true congregation in which the Lord came to dwell in Old Testament

---

[6] Kevin J. Conner The Tabernacle of Moses pg.12

times…There were not to be divisions within the congregation."[7]

The Sanctuary (Exodus 25:8). The word sanctuary means "a holy place" or "place set apart." It was the place for the habitation of a holy God. We who are born-again believers are the sanctuary of God the Holy Spirit. Because of Christ's work of redemption, we have to be set apart for His habitation.

The Tent of Testimony or Witness (Numbers 9:15; 17:7; 18:2). Conner states: "The Tabernacle received this title because it contained the Ark of the Covenant which contained the tables of the law. The tables of the law were called the 'testimony' of a holy God. They were His moral standard for redeemed Israel."[8]

This speaks of "…Christ, who is the faithful witness…" (Rev. 1:5). The one who comes in the

---

[7] Theodore H. Epp Portraits of Christ in Tabernacle pg.27
[8] Kevin J. Conner The Tabernacle of Moses pg.9

The Tabernacle a Revelation of Jesus Christ

volume of the book (Hebrews 10:7). Jesus said "Search the scriptures; for in them ye think ye have eternal life: and they are they which testify of me" (John 5:39).

The Tabernacle was also referred to as the House of God; the Tent; Tabernacle of the Lord; and a host of names and titles which all point to one thing that this was the Divinely chosen place where God chose to dwell amongst His chosen people.

Chapter 2
The Outer Court
A view from the Outside

The tabernacle consisted of two compartments: The Holy place and the Holy of Holies; surrounded by a third compartment known as the Outer Court. This last compartment is where God met man. This is the demarcation point, no one could be accepted unless they approached God first, through the outer court.

The outer court was 100 cubits long (150 feet long) and 50 cubits wide (75 feet wide). It was an open area surrounded by a hanging of fine twined linen, supported by 60 pillars (20 each on the north and south sides and 10 each on the east and west sides). Each pillar stood in a foundation of brass (bronze). Each had a crown or chaptier of silver. For the sinner the first glimpses of the tabernacle is the outer court; here we see the 60 pillars overlaid with bronze, which supported a wall of fine linen 5 cubits high; according to Levy this wall was approximately 7 1/2 feet high and 7 1/2 feet apart.[9]

---

[9] David M. Levy The Tabernacle: Shadows of the Messiah pg.20

The Tabernacle a Revelation of Jesus Christ

The pillars configured a rectangle shape, which were inserted into sockets of bronze which were buried into the sand or ground. These pillars were fastened into place by cords attached to the top of the pillars; these cords were made of goats hair; and at the other end a bronze stake driven into the ground.

The pillars were held together by silver connecting rods, on which the linen curtains were hung by silver hooks. Anyone on the outside viewing this structure would be witnessing something awesome. Epp, however disagrees stating: "From the outside, the tabernacle was unattractive, but there was breathtaking beauty on the inside."[10] We must remember that for the individual viewing the tabernacle from without, would see the linen wall of white, the pillars crowned with sliver, and the door with its artistic work. The seeker would also witness the smoke from the burnt offerings, that were offered continually upon the altar. The seeker would also witness the fire by night and a pillar of cloud

---

[10] Theodore H. Epp <u>Portraits of Christ in the Tabernacle</u> pg.17

by day, seeing this would attract anyone even the skeptic.

As a seeker views the pillars, the linen wall, the silver and the bronze he cannot help but wonder what does all this mean and approaching the tabernacle, his curiosity would be satisfied. We would come to understand the pillars overlaid with bronze represents judgment, it's symbolic of God's righteous judgment. As for the pillars themselves we are not told what they are made of; nonetheless Levy says: they were "made of acacia wood."[11] But scripture does not reveal what they were made of, only that they were overlaid with bronze and set in sockets of bronze. What should be clear is what the bronze represents and that is judgment, not man's, but God's righteous judgment. Jesus said: judge not according to the appearance, but judge righteous judgment (John 7:24). He was implying that we needed to judge according to God's standards not our lowly self-centered standards. 2 Timothy 4:8; tells us that Jesus Christ is the "Lord the righteous

---

[11] David M. Levy The Tabernacle Shadows of the Messiah pg.20

The Tabernacle a Revelation of Jesus Christ

judge." Let us not miss Christ to whom all things in the tabernacle points to and represents.

As our eyes witness the righteous judgment of God we gaze upon the silver crowns on top of the bronze pillars, and the silver connecting rods on which the curtains hung, on silver hooks, pointing to our redeemer. Silver is symbolic of redemption. It represents our redemption through the blood of Jesus Christ. The linen curtains were hung on silver connecting rods by silver hooks. The curtains enclosed the tabernacle forming the outer court. It was a wall about seven and a half feet high making it impossible for anyone to climb over. Signifying that there was only one way to enter. The linen emphatically represents righteousness, not our righteousness which is as "filthy rags." But the righteousness of God, which we can only attain through acceptance of Jesus as our savior. Anything else falls short of God's requirements, which are "just" for He is "Righteousness;" not because of anything He has achieved or does, but because, He was, is and shall always be righteous because He "changes not." Righteousness is a divine attribute and, therefore, He cannot be anything else but righteous, and, therefore, must demand that anyone who desires to approach Him must see and receive His righteousness for there is no other way to enter into the tabernacle of God's presence unless we see Him as He is and that is Holy, and righteous, there is no other way.

The Door to the Court

"And thou shalt make the court of the tabernacle" (Exodus 27:9).

If the seeker sought to enter into the court, there was only one entrance, and that was through the Door of the court. There was only one prescribed way. Although the curtain was a barrier between the people and God, which implied keep back. Access to God was possible through the Door. The door points to Jesus Christ who is the "Way;" anyone else, "are thieves and robbers." The Door makes a statement: whomsoever will come, let them come and receive the salvation of the Lord.

As we witness the glory of the fine twined linen, we are brought to the beauty and splendor of the door. The door of the court is given at least three names which are: The Gate (Exodus 27:16); The Curtain for the Door of the Court (Numbers 3:26); and the Door of the court (Numbers 32:6). The gate signified the one way of approach to the tabernacle proper. The linen faced anyone approaching the tabernacle. Conner states: "These linen curtains told man to keep out, but if a man would follow the curtains he would in every case come to the Gate. The gate spoke a different message. The gate said that man could enter, but only God's way."[12]

There are four things that became apparent about the gate:

• This is the only entrance to the court.

---

[12] Kevin J. Conner The Tabernacle of Moses pg.79

The Tabernacle a Revelation of Jesus Christ

• The gate was wide enough to accommodate everyone that wanted to come into the tabernacle (according to Epp the gate was thirty feet wide[13]).

• It was a beautiful gate inwrought with, blue, purple, scarlet and fine linen, made it something that was attractive to all.

• The gate was distinctive no one could've mistaken it for the linen wall. The colors made it stand out from the linen; all who saw it knew it was the only legal entrance into the court and the very presence of God. The gate typifies Jesus as the only way to salvation: "I am the way, the truth, and the life: no man cometh unto the Father, but by me."(John 14:6);"Neither is there salvation in any other; for there is none other name under heaven given among men, whereby we must be saved." (Acts 4:12). Conner affirms: The fine twined linen in the gate typified Christ in the Gospel of Luke as the Perfect Man the Righteous One, He who knew no sin but became sin for us. The blue typifies Christ in the Gospel of John as the Eternal Son of God or He who came from heaven (The Heavenly One).

---

[13] Theodore H. Epp Portraits of Christ in the Tabernacle pg.64

The Tabernacle a Revelation of Jesus Christ

The purple depicts Christ as King, the Royal One, who Matthew writes about. The scarlet foreshadows Christ as the perfect sacrifice who is the theme of the Gospel of Mark.[14]

All of these colors inwrought in the door together delivers an astonishing picture of the Lord Jesus Christ, that cannot be overlooked; He is the perfect example. Looking at the gate and its colors we get a glimpse of what God's presence is like on the other side. The gate was designed to draw the seeker into the court. Although this must have been breathtaking, let us not forget that there is more of God to receive on the other side of the gate.

Before we venture on it is noteworthy to mention that the gate of the
court was five cubits high and twenty cubits wide. These measurements Conner points out were one hundred square, the same area as the Door of the Tabernacle, and the Veil to the Holy of Holies; he

---

[14] Kevin J. Conner Op. cit., pg.79

says: When this is seen alone it speaks of total commitment to God."[15]

The gate was upheld by four pillars in sockets of brass. These four were a part of the sixty pillars that made up the outer court. Conner states: "The pillars are significant of the worldwide availability of the Gate."[16]

The Brazen Alter

"And thou shalt make an altar of shittim wood, five cubits long, and five cubits broad; the altar shall be foursquare: and the height thereof shall be three cubits. And thou shalt make the horns of it upon the four corners thereof: his horns shall be of the same: and thou shalt overlay it with brass." (Exodus 27:1-2).

Once we pass through the gate, we now draw our attention to the Brazen Altar. The word brazen means: brass which denotes judgment. The word

---

[15] Kevin J. Conner Ibid., pg.80
[16] Loc. Cit.

The Tabernacle a Revelation of Jesus Christ

Altar means: "slaughter place." It also means "lifted up" or "high" or "ascending."[17]

This was the place of sacrifice, a place of death, a place where the innocent died for the guilty; the substitution was made here and only here. Notice the position of the piece of furniture it was the farthest point possible from the presence of God, and at the point of entry for the seeker of God.

According to Epp "If a man endeavored to approach God without a substitute, it meant certain death."[18] The seeker must take care of business here first, before proceeding any further. Sin had to be dealt with, "For the wages of sin is death; but the gift of God is eternal life through Jesus Christ our Lord." (Romans 6:23). This was only done through sacrifice on the brazen altar, this was a foreshadow of the cross on which the Lord Jesus would shed His blood for the sin of the world. The altar was made of acacia (also known as shittim) wood, which came from a tree that grew in the desert under bitter conditions, it was white, durable, incorruptible. This

---

[17] Shelia Reynolds Lecture "The Tabernacle" pg.68
[18] Theodore H. Epp Portraits of Christ in the Tabernacle pg.68

The Tabernacle a Revelation of Jesus Christ

pictured Jesus in His humanity. "In His humanity, Christ lived under the most serve conditions and gave His life in a horrible death on the cross."[19]

"So, Christ was once offered to bear the sins of many; and unto them that look for him shall he appear the second time without sin unto salvation." (Hebrews 9:28). The altar was five cubits long, and five cubits wide, and three cubits high and was four square with four horns. Reynolds states: "The number 5 denotes God's grace and the number 3 points us to the Godhead."[20] The horns speak of salvation, strength and power and was also used to bind the unwilling sacrifices. The horns of the altar are those which were touched by the blood on the day of atonement. The four horns also speak of: redemption; ransom; substitution; and reconciliation, this is the primary message of the altar. There was fire upon the altar perpetually, it was not a man made or strange fire (Leviticus 10:1 3), the penalty for such an act was death (Leviticus 10:1-2). "This fire was a type of God's consuming

---

[19] Shelia Reynolds Lecture "The Tabernacle" pg.33
[20] Shelia Reynolds Ibid., pg.33

fire of judgment that came upon Christ (the Sacrificial Lamb) as He hung on the cross (the Altar). He paid the penalty of sin for you and I. No man could have taken His life. He, Himself, laid it down."[21]

The Brazen Laver

Moses was instructed to make a laver which was to be set in the Court Yard between the tent of the congregation and the Brazen Altar (Exodus 40:7, 30). The Hebrew word for laver is, "Kiyyor," which means pots or pans.[22]

The laver was made out of solid brass, nothing concerning the size or design has been recorded. What we do know is, that the brass came from the looking glasses of the women. "And he made the laver of brass, and the foot of it of brass, of the looking glasses of the women assembling, which

---

[21] Shelia Reynolds Op.. cit., pg.35
[22] Shelia Reynolds Op. cit., pg.36

The Tabernacle a Revelation of Jesus Christ

assembled at the door of the tabernacle of the congregation." (Exodus 38:8). The laver was for cleansing. The priests were to wash here before they could proceed into the tabernacle. The brazen altar represented judgment against sin, it is where man receives justification from sin. The brazen laver represented judgment against self, it is where man is sanctified from self, unto the Lord. The Tabernacle represented the place of fellowship with God, and no one can enter into fellowship except he cleansed himself.

The water in the laver was symbolic of the Word of God. The scripture declares that the new birth comes through the Word. The scripture often speaks of cleansing through the Word (John 17:17). "Wherewithal shall a young man cleanse his way? by taking heed thereto according to thy word." (Psalms 119:9). The priests were instructed to wash their hands and feet at the laver. This had spiritual symbolism. The hands speak of our service to the Lord. Clean feet refer to our walk before a Holy God. "I therefore, the prisoner of the Lord, beseech

The Tabernacle a Revelation of Jesus Christ

you that ye walk worthy of the vocation wherewith ye are called…" (Ephesians 4:1). All priests had to wash at the laver before ministering any service. This is symbolic of our service to Christ, we must be cleansed by the water, which is the "Word made flesh." Our daily contact with the world demands a daily washing by the Word.

Chapter 3

The Tabernacle

After we have basked in all the glories of the Outer Court, it is imperative that we don't let the beauties thereof to allow us to become overwhelmed, that we think we have obtained it all (Philippians 3:12). But let's press on for the goal which is yet before us. In the outer court we recognize our need for salvation. At the brazen altar, a substitutionary offering is made for our sin. And after sin has been satisfactorily paid for, we see ourselves in the laver and begin to wash with the water therein and sanctification takes place.

And now we come to the Door of the Tabernacle where only a few can enter into the Holy Place. At the gate we see the seeker, at the door we see the believer. It is only the believers who can stand before the Door of the Tabernacle or even think of entering through the door into the Holy Place.

Before we enter into the Holy Place, let us take a look at the tabernacle (building) structure. The Tabernacle consisted of two compartments or

The Tabernacle a Revelation of Jesus Christ

rooms known as the Holy Place, into which the priests were permitted in The Tabernacle a Revelation of Jesus Christ to minister the priestly office; and the Holy of Holies or the Most Holy Place which the high priest entered into once a year, on the Day of Atonement. The tabernacle consisted of 48 boards of shittim wood overlaid with gold. The shittim wood is a type of the sinless character, life and humanity of Jesus Christ. The gold represents His divine nature or His divinity.[23]

The actual arrangement of the 48 boards were: 20 boards on the Southside; 20 boards on the north side; 6 boards on the west side and 2 boards for the conners on the west end, making a total of 48 boards. These boards formed one tabernacle. Each board measured 10 cubits high and 1 1/2 cubits wide. According to Conner: "All the boards were to measure up to this Divine Standard in order to qualify as a Board in God's Tabernacle."[24] Conner also states that: "Every Christian must measure up

---

[23] Shelia Reynolds Op. cit., pg.13
[24] Kevin J. Conner Op. cit., pg.55

34

The Tabernacle a Revelation of Jesus Christ

to the Standard of the pattern Son, the Lord Jesus Christ.[25] This is a type of the Church structure as God intended it to be. "Till we all come in the unity of the faith, and of the knowledge of the Son of God, unto a perfect The Tabernacle a Revelation of Jesus Christ man, unto the measure of the stature of the fulness of Christ…" (Ephesians 4:13).

Each board was inserted into 96 sockets of silver, 40 sockets for the twenty boards on the south side, 40 for the north side, 16 sockets for the 8 boards on the west side, all totaling 96 sockets in all. The silver being symbolic of redemption, atonement and the price of a soul; the foundation of the Church in the wilderness. "For other foundation can no man lay than that is laid, which is Jesus Christ." (1 Corinthians 3:11). All the boards were consolidated into the whole by 15 bars made of shittim wood overlaid with gold, there were five bars each that passed through rings of gold around the outside of the boards binding them together into one structure.

---

[25] Loc. Cit.

The Tabernacle a Revelation of Jesus Christ

Here we see a type of the Church "Fitly framed together" (Ephesians 2:21; 4:16).

The Tabernacle building was 45ft. Long, 15ft. wide and 15ft. high. The first room of the Tabernacle is symbolic of or is the place of spiritual fellowship with God.[26] The second room of the Tabernacle called the Holy of Holies, or the Most Holy Place, was the place of "special worship."[27]

There were four pieces of furniture placed within the Tabernacle. In the Holy Place there were three pieces of furniture: the Golden Lampstand which was placed on the southside of the Tabernacle (Exodus 25:31), directly across from the Lampstand on the northside was the Table of Shewbread, which was made of shittim wood overlaid with gold (Exodus 25:23-24). Also within the room was an altar, to burn incense upon, this too was made of shittim wood, and this too was overlaid with gold, and placed in the west end of the Holy Place just before the Veil (Exodus 30:1-3, 6).

---

[26] Theodore H. Epp <u>Op. cit.,</u> pg.85
[27] <u>Op. cit.,</u>

The Tabernacle a Revelation of Jesus Christ

In the Most Holy Place there was one piece of furniture; the Ark of the Covenant, also made of shittim wood and overlaid with gold (Exodus 25:17). The Tabernacle a Revelation of Jesus Christ The beauty of the Tabernacle structure and all its furnishings were not visible from the outside. It was only visible through our actions at the Brazen Altar, the Brazen Laver and the Tabernacle Door.

There were four coverings that constituted the Tabernacle roof and ceiling. These four coverings protected the contents, and anyone within the Tabernacle.

Moreover, thou shalt make the tabernacle with ten curtains of fine twined linen, and blue, and purple, and scarlet: with cherubims of cunning work shalt thou make them. And thou shalt make curtains of goats' hair to be a covering upon the tabernacle: eleven curtains shalt thou make. And thou shalt make a covering for the tent of rams' skins dyed red, and a covering above of badgers' skins. (Exodus 26:1,7,14).

The Tabernacle a Revelation of Jesus Christ

From the outside we see the covering of badgers skin. From the inside we would see the curtains of fine linen. The fine linen was placed directly over the frame work of the Tabernacle, this comprised the actual ceiling of the sanctuary.[28]

Above the linen was a covering of goat's hair, directly above the curtain of goat's hair lay a covering of rams skin dyed red. These four coverings "Typified Christ as the protection both of God's perfect Holiness and to man's perfect standing in Christ.[29] Epp and Levy suggest that the outer covering of badgers skin, were not badgers skin as we know them, but rather a "porpoise skin," a marine animal plentiful in the region, placed on top.[30] The skins were very durable, it provided, "perfect protection against the elements of the desert."[31] Hebershon disagrees with both Epp and Levy, and believes that the actual kind of skin is uncertain.[32]

---

[28] Kevin J. Conner Op. cit., pg.61
[29] Theodore H. Epp Op. cit., pg.90
[30] David M. Levy Op. cit., pg.21
[31] Theodore H. Epp Op. cit., pg.90-91
[32] Ada R. Habershon, Outline Studies of the Tabernacle pg.33

The Tabernacle a Revelation of Jesus Christ

The second covering or covering beneath the badgers skin was the Rams skin dyed red. It was not visible to anyone on the outside or the inside, but was needed for further protection of the Tabernacle.[33] The ram skin speaks of Christ the substitute through death.[34] The Ram was used in the trespass offering (Leviticus 5:15), Burnt offerings (Leviticus 8:18) and Peace offerings (Leviticus (:4). Genesis 22:8-13 gives us our first account with the Ram as a substitutionary offering,

"And Abraham went and took the ram, and offered him up for a burnt offering in the stead of his son". But Christ is now our only substitute for sin. "So, Christ was once offered to bear the sins of many; and unto them that look for him shall he appear the second time without sin unto salvation." (Hebrews 9:28).

The rams skin were to be dyed red; this is symbolic of sacrificial blood and can be identified with

---

[33] Theodore H. Epp, Op. cit., pg.92
[34] Shelia Reynolds, Op. cit., pg.39

cleansing for sin. According to Conner: "this covering was central to the Tabernacle pointing to the central figure of the Godhead, the Lord Jesus Christ."[35]

"The covering God provided was evidence of His grace and love. God would have been completely righteous in showing no mercy at all, but instead, He provided a covering."[36]

Thank you Lord for your Grace and Mercy!

"And thou shalt make curtains of goats' hair to be a covering upon the tabernacle: eleven curtains shalt thou make." (Exodus 26:7). The covering of Goats hair was underneath the covering of rams skin. This covering made of goats hair was actually eleven curtains which formed one curtain. Six curtains joined together in the front, the sixth being doubled over the entrance, and five curtains at the back.[37] The goats hair represents "Christ as the sin offering."[38]

[35] Kevin J. Conner, Op. cit., pg.65
[36] Theodore H. Epp, Op. cit., pg.93
[37] Ada R. Habershon, Op. cit., pg.32
[38] Theodore H. Epp, Op. cit., pg.94

The Tabernacle a Revelation of Jesus Christ

The goat symbolized the fact that Jesus Christ has removed our sins. When we as a seeker become a believer and put our trust in Christ as savior, the penalty of his or her sin is paid forever, and there is no more condemnation (Romans 8:1).

The fourth, or inner covering of the tabernacle was made of "fine twined linen." "Moreover, thou shalt make the tabernacle with ten curtains of fine twined linen, and blue, and purple, and scarlet: with cherubims of cunning work shalt thou make them." (Exodus 26:1). This covering consisted of ten curtains joined together in two sets of five; these curtains were joined together by 50 taches of gold and 100 loops of blue, the fine twined linen, blue, purple and scarlet; and embroidered with Cherubim. These typified the character and glories of the Lord Jesus Christ.[39] When the tabernacle was erected this was the first covering placed over the tabernacle. Mr. Epp suggests that the exterior covering was unattractive, this interior covering was beautiful. We can only realize Christ's true beauty on the

---

[39] Ada R. Habershon, Op. cit., pg.31

inside.[40] The fine linen which was embroidered with figures of cherubim in blue, purple, and scarlet. Epp declares:

This linen represented Christ in all His glory and perfect righteousness. The white the sinless, righteous Christ. The blue represents His heavenly origin or nature. Scarlet His sacrificial death. Purple a combination of blue and scarlet represents His royal character; His kingly and sovereign nature and stately splendor.[41]

Reynolds sums it up this way: "fine linen speaks of Christ's perfect life as seen in all his functions: as King, Servant, Perfect Man and Perfect God."[42]

Habershon alludes that the colors in the linen points us to the four gospels in the New Testament she writes that:

> In Matthew's Gospel the Lord is represented as the Son of David—the scarlet. In Mark we see Him as the perfect Servant—the fine twined linen. In Luke He is the Son of Man—the one who will wear

---

[40] Theodore H. Epp, Op. cit., pg.96
[41] Loc. Cit.
[42] Shelia Reynolds, Op. cit., pg39

The Tabernacle a Revelation of Jesus Christ

the many crowns, (Revelation 19:12, 16)—
the purple. In John we see Him as the Son
of God—the blue, the heavenly color.[43]

These same colors are also used in the Veil, the
hanging of the door of the Tabernacle, and the gate
of the court. There was no cherubim mentioned in
the description of the gate and the door. All three
hangings says; Habershon were equal in area.[44]

In scripture we see cherubim as guardians (Genesis
3:24) of the Holiness of God. In the linen covering
the cherubim with outstretched wings were woven
into the linen, hovering over the priests as they
ministered. The cherubim represented protection
given to those in the Tabernacle.[45]

Those who remain on the outside of the tabernacle
which is a type of Christ will not see any of the
beauty or the symbolism of the protecting hand of
God. " But the natural man receiveth not the things
of the Spirit of God: for they are foolishness unto
him: neither can he know them, because they are

---

[43] Ada R. Habershon, Op. cit., pg.32
[44] Loc. Cit.
[45] Theodore H. Epp, Op. cit., pg.96

43

spiritually discerned." (1 Corinthians 2:14). "But if our gospel be hid, it is hid to them that are lost: In whom the god of this world hath blinded the minds of them which believe not, lest the light of the glorious gospel of Christ, who is the image of God, should shine unto them." (2 Corinthians 4:3-4).

Let us, not be satisfied with salvation at the altar but let us seek the inner walls of the sanctuary where true fellowship begins. I agree with Epp who says: We will be different individuals when we truly see the glory of God. The more time we spend on the inside of the sanctuary, the more we will behold and appreciate His beauty.[46]

---

[46] Ibid., pg.96

Chapter 4

The Door to the Holy Place

"And thou shalt make an hanging for the door of the tent, of blue, and purple, and scarlet, and fine twined linen, wrought with needlework. And thou shalt make for the hanging five pillars of shittim wood, and overlay them with gold, and their hooks shall be of gold: and thou shalt cast five sockets of brass for them." (Exodus 26:36-37).

As the seeker enters into the outer court, and makes a commitment at the brazen altar, his or her life is immediately transformed from seeker to believer (John 3:3:16-17, Romans 10:9-10). This typifies the commitment we make to Christ at calvary's cross. The believer, standing at the Door must now make another decision, he must decide whether he will be satisfied with the altar and laver experience of salvation and sanctification, or will he experience the spiritual fellowship beyond the beauty of the Door. Jesus said: "I am the way, the truth, and the life: no man cometh unto the Father, but by me." (John 14:6).

The Tabernacle a Revelation of Jesus Christ

The door to the tabernacle was not a door suspended upon hinges, but was actually a curtain hung upon five pillars of shittim wood covered with gold. Throughout scripture the door is referred to as: "an hanging for the door of the tent" (Exodus 26:36-37), "the hanging" (Exodus 26:37), and "an hanging for the tabernacle door" (Exodus 36:37).

Some scholars such as Theodore H. Epp refers to it as "The Door of the Holy Place."[47] Whatever terminology, we may use they all refer to the beautiful curtain "of blue, purple, scarlet and fine twined linen," which served as a barrier to all, except the priests, who were permitted access in and out of the Holy Place.

The door represented Christ, who is the only "way...unto the Father" (John 14:6). It was hung upon pillars of shittim wood covered with gold. These materials being significant of His humanity and His deity. The wood was a non-decaying wood which was found in the desert, which endured

---

[47] Theodore H. Epp, Op. cit., pg.99

The Tabernacle a Revelation of Jesus Christ

the harshness of its environment, which was typical of the ministry of Christ on earth. He endured every test as a man was found without one sin (1 Peter 2:22-24). The gold was symbolic of His deity (Hebrews 1:8-9). The combination of the two says Epp: "speaks of Christ as the God-Man."[48]

Conner offers this suggestion concerning the significance of the pillars:

> Upholding this Door, there were five pillars. Five is the number of the Grace of God...the number five surely spoke of the five books of the Law given to Moses...Isaiah receives a revelation of a glorious five-fold name of Christ...(Isa. 9:6)...To the New Testament Church the number five has special meaning. The New Testament Church is given the fivefold ministry of Apostle, Prophet, Evangelist, Pastor and Teacher (Eph. 4:9-16). It is their responsibility to uphold the Lord Jesus as the Grace of God. Five is the number of the New Testament writers of the Epistles-

---

[48] Ibid., pg.102

The Tabernacle a Revelation of Jesus Christ

> Peter, James, John, Jude and Paul. These were indeed pillars in the early Church, upholding the glorious person of the Son of God and the revelation of truth pertains to the New Testament Church (Gal. 2:8-9).[49]

"And he made an hanging for the tabernacle door of blue, and purple, and scarlet, and fine twined linen, of needlework…" (Exodus 36:37). The blue, purple, and scarlet, and fine linen represented four aspects of the life of Christ. The blue is the color of heaven, signifying that Christ is the Lord from heaven, who satisfied all the demands of God. Purple is the color of royalty emphasizing Christ is the "KING OF KINGS, AND LORD OF LORDS."(Rev. 19:16), the royal man, our kinsman redeemer. The scarlet represents the sacrificial blood on calvary's cross, He is the sacrificial man, the one who "laid down his life for us…" (1 John 3:16). The fine linen speaks to us of His righteousness, "The LORD is righteous in all his ways, and holy in all his works." (Psalms 145:17).

---

[49] Kevin J. Conner, Op. cit., pg.70-71

The Tabernacle a Revelation of Jesus Christ

The pillars were set in foundations of brass. As previously stated brass speaks of judgment. According to Epp: These pillars pointed towards the complete judgment of Christ, and thus they upheld the inviting curtains of entrance made possible by His finished work on Calvary. So, they remind the worshipper that Christ is the door..." (John 14:6).[50]

The purpose of the Door was to provide easy and frequent access for the priest to minister before the Lord daily, within the Holy Place. Only the priests who entered through the door beheld the glory within, those who remained in the outer court saw only those colors intermingled in the Door. Soltau suggests:

That this may be intended as a lesson, "to teach that every worshipper of God recognizes the beauty and perfection's of Christ, as God manifest in the flesh, his eyes rests upon the door-curtain. But nearer we approach to God as priests, the more intimate our fellowship with Him.[51]

---

[50] Theodore H. Epp, Op. cit., pg.102
[51] Henry W. Soltau, The Tabernacle the Priesthood and the Offerings pg.69-70

The Tabernacle a Revelation of Jesus Christ

Chapter 5

The Golden Lampstand

And thou shalt make a candlestick of pure gold: of beaten work shall the candlestick be made: his shaft, and his branches, his bowls, his knops, and his flowers, shall be of the same. And six branches shall come out of the sides of it; three branches of the candlestick out of the one side, and three branches of the candlestick out of the other side: Three bowls made like unto almonds, with a knop and a flower in one branch; and three bowls made like almonds in the other branch, with a knop and a flower: so, in the six branches that come out of the candlestick. And in the candlestick shall be four bowls made like unto almonds, with their knops and their flowers. And there shall be a knop under two branches of the same, and a knop under two branches of the same, and a knop under two branches of the same, according to the six branches that proceed out of the candlestick. Their knops and their branches shall be of the same: all it shall be one beaten work of pure gold. And thou shalt make the seven lamps thereof:

and they shall light the lamps thereof, that they may give light over against it. And the tongs thereof, and the snuffdishes thereof, shall be of pure gold. Of a talent of pure gold shall he make it, with all these vessels. And look that thou make them after their pattern, which was shewed thee in the mount. (Exodus 25:31-40).

As we pass through the Door of the Tabernacle, we enter into the first room or compartment of the Tabernacle, called the Holy Place. Upon entering into the Holy Place (which measured 30ft long by 15ft wide[52]), the priest would see three articles of furniture, and the veil of fine-twined linen (also embroidered with cherubim). He could only witness all the glories of the Holy Place because of the illuminating light of the golden lampstand.

We can only imagine what this might have been like. It had to be an awesome sight to behold the light of the lampstand casting its glow upon everything within the Holy Place. Just imagine for

---

[52] David m> Levy, Op. cit., pg.41

a moment, how this light reflected upon the table of pure gold, and upon the golden altar of incense. This must've been an awesome sight within the Holy Place, with the light from the lampstand piercing through the smoke ascending from the altar, and bouncing back towards the priests from the boards overlaid with gold, and off of the ceiling with its embroidered cherubim, and the veil, which divided the Holy Place from the Most Holy Place. And if he were to turn around, the glorious colors of the door would also be beautifully illuminated. Combining all of this, must've projected a breathtaking sight. This could be nothing short of the glory of God being manifested in the place of spiritual fellowship. ("And without controversy great is the mystery of godliness: God was manifest…" 1 Timothy 3:16). How spectacular was this room with all the rays of light being reflected by all the gold, all the colors, the smoke, and even the priestly garments. This must have presented a picture that was comparable to nothing on earth. Well said the writer of Hebrews: "Who being the brightness of his

The Tabernacle a Revelation of Jesus Christ

glory, and the express image of his person..."
(Hebrews 1:3). The light from the lampstand cast its
light throughout the Holy Place, allowing all who
entered in to see Christ revealed. "Then spake
Jesus...I am the light of the world: he that followeth
me shall not walk in darkness, but shall have the
light of life." (John 8:12).

The Tabernacle had no windows that would allow
light in or out. The only source of light was the
lampstand made of pure gold. "There was no
dimensions given, but its size, weight and beauty
portray Christ in His fathomless greatness."[53]

The lampstand itself contained rich symbolic
teaching for both the Christian and Non-Christian.
The gold in the lampstand speaks of the deity of
Christ, the divine and only begotten Son of God,
who stepped down, out of eternity into time and
clothed Himself in a garment of flesh, became
100% Man and 100% God. "...Without blemish and
without spot..." (1 Peter 1:19).

---

[53] David M. Levy, Op. cit., pg.42

The Tabernacle a Revelation of Jesus Christ

The purpose of the lampstand was to provide light within the Holy Place, so that all the priests who entered would walk by the light (1 John 1:5-6), it speaks of Christ as the light of the world. Christ is the one who lights up the walk and fellowship of the believer.

This truth has a frightening contrast; as the light of the lampstand shined brightly inside, anyone on the outside couldn't see the light and therefore, were blinded to the light of life. Any who were unworthy or hesitant could not receive the pleasures of this divine fellowship with God which was only obtainable inside the Holy Place, under the light of the lampstand.

This fellowship was only for the priests who ministered before the Lord. This is a type of the priesthood believer, who has a right of fellowship with God through the finished work of Jesus Christ. For "...we are a chosen generation, a royal priesthood, an holy nation, a peculiar people; that ye (we) should shew forth the praises of him who has called you (us) out of darkness into his marvelous

The Tabernacle a Revelation of Jesus Christ

light." (1 Peter 2:9). Only those who sincerely seek the true fellowship of Christ, will experience the illumination of His truth and Holiness. Our fellowship or intimacy with Christ depends solely upon us. He has made the way possible, now it is up to you and I, whether we choose His way (walking in the light of the Holy Place), or be satisfied with our current standing. We are always as close to God as we want to be. For God has already provided the only way into His presence, through Jesus Christ (John 14:6).

The lampstand was made of pure gold, of beaten or hammered work, as commanded by God (Exodus 25:31). This typified Christ who was "Despised and rejected…was wounded for our transgressions, he was bruised for our iniquities" (Isaiah 53:3,5). It was not assembled together by pieces, but, was one solid block of gold. The gold according to Levy weighed 90 pounds.[54]

A.B. Simpson measures the value of "A talent of gold [worth close to $1 million in 1985

---

[54] David M. Levy, Op. cit., pg.41

The Tabernacle a Revelation of Jesus Christ

money]…"[55] ($3,298,221 in today's money). Here we see that God will always provide His servants with whatever's necessary to complete the task at hand.

The lampstand stood not only for Christ and the Holy Spirit, but it is also symbolic of the Church and the Christian. It represents the believer as the reflectors of His light. It typifies us as the sevenfold, complete light- bearers who are reflecting this light to the dark world around us and so we become the lights of the world (Matthew 5:14-16).

There were six branches which came out of the side of the lampstand. None from the front. The center branch which was not of the six, came out of the top of the shaft. "Six is the number of man…These six branches portray man redeemed; and yet above them is the seventh branch-the Perfect Man, the Man Christ Jesus.[56]

---

[55] A.B. Simpson, Christin the Tabernacle pg.53
[56] C.W. Slemming, Op. cit., pg.123-124

The Tabernacle a Revelation of Jesus Christ

Seven represents divine completeness. And we are complete in Him (Colossians 4:12).

As has been previously stated, the purpose of the lampstand was to give light, typifying the purpose of the church to reflect that light. It isn't the lamp that made the light but only bore it. The light was supplied by the oil that was constantly put into the lamp.

Ada Habershon offers this explanation concerning the oil, it was:

A type of the ministry on earth of the power of the Holy Spirit (the oil), having Christ for its source and subject." "The branches by themselves had no standing in the sanctuary; separated from the center shaft they cease to be light-bearers." The oil is "for light." The Holy Spirit is given to us that we may shine for God.[57]

The Holy Spirit on the day of Pentecost was poured out upon the church (Acts 2:1,4), before Pentecost

---

[57] Ada R. Habershon, Op. cit., pg.47

The Tabernacle a Revelation of Jesus Christ

He descended upon Christ-the center lamp, after He was baptized in the Jordan river (Luke 3:22). Today the Spirit manifests in the church the true knowledge of Christ, the light of the world. The priests replenished the lamps daily. So has God filled us with His Holy Spirit, so we can daily"…shew forth the praises of him who hath called you out of darkness into his marvelous light…" (1 Peter 2:9).

Chapter 6

The Table of Showbread

"Thou shalt also make a table of shittim wood: two cubits shall be the length thereof, and a cubit the breadth thereof, and a cubit and a half the height thereof. And thou shalt overlay it with pure gold, and make thereto a crown of gold round about. And thou shalt make unto it a border of an hand breadth round about, and thou shalt make a golden crown to the border thereof round about. And thou shalt make for it four rings of gold, and put the rings in the four corners that are on the four feet thereof. Over against the border shall the rings be for places of the staves to bear the table.

And thou shalt make the staves of shittim wood, and overlay them with gold, that the table may be borne with them. And thou shalt make the dishes thereof, and spoons thereof, and covers thereof, and bowls thereof, to cover withal: of pure gold shalt thou make them. And thou shalt set upon the table shewbread before me alway." (Exodus 25:23-30).

The Tabernacle a Revelation of Jesus Christ

Once again we hear the commandment from God, "Thou shalt…make." His instruction to Moses were specific, it was to be made of shittim wood, and covered with gold, a crown of gold encircled it. Gold rings were made for the four corners where, two staves also of shittim wood covered with

gold were also placed to transport the table. The table measurements were: "Three feet long, and one and a half feet wide, and two and three-tenths feet high."[58]

The table of Showbread symbolized the life and ministry of the Lord. A.B. Simpson relates:

> The purpose of the table was to exhibit the bread. This is what the church and ministry are appointed to do…It had but one use: not to show itself but the bread…ministry is out of place when its brilliancy obscures the Savior…The table was for the purpose of holding forth the bread as an offering for God as well for the priests to use. So, the highest aim in all our ministry should be to hold Christ forth for God's glory…"[59]

Our purpose in Christ is always to manifest the praises of Him, who has called, chosen and prepared

---

[58] David M. Levy, Op. cit., pg.71
[59] A.B. Simpson, OP. cit., pg.71

us to stand in His marvelous light. It is not in the believer's position to seek any glory of his or her own, but to stand in the place where Christ has positioned them that they can display the bread of life. As the light of (the lampstand) Jesus shines upon each and every believer (loaf). The table covered in gold symbolizes Jesus' deity. The wood spoke of His humanity. When the two are combined, the wood and the gold together typifies, the union of Jesus' divine and human natures. "Who, being in the form of God, thought it not robbery to be equal with God: But made himself of no reputation, and took upon him the form of a servant, and was made in the likeness of men." (Philippians 2:6-7). C.I. Scofield offers this observation:

...Nothing in this passage teaches the Eternal Word (John 1:1) emptied Himself of either His divine nature, or His attributes, but only of the outward and visible manifestation of the Godhead. "He emptied,

The Tabernacle a Revelation of Jesus Christ

stripped Himself of the insignia of Majesty." "When occasion demanded He exercised His divine attributes…"[60]

Scofield continues:

The deity of Christ is declared in scripture: (I) In intimations and explicit predictions of the O.T. (a) The theophanies intimate the appearance of God in human form, and His ministry thus to man (Gen. 16:7-13, 18:2-23).

(b) The Messiah is expressly declared to be the Son of God (Psa. 2:2-9), and God (Psa. 45:6,7; Heb. 1:8,9). (c) His virgin birth was foretold as the means through which God could be "Immanuel," God with us (Isa. 7:13,14; Mt. 2:6; 1:22,23)…(f) His eternal being is declared (Mic. 5:2; Mt. 2:6; John 7:42)… (2) Christ Himself affirmed His deity. (a) He applied Himself Jehovistic I AM. (John 8:24,56-58. The Jews correctly understood this to be our Lord's claim to full deity [v.59]., John 10:33; 17:4-6)… (3) The N.T. writers ascribe titles to Christ (John 1:1; 20:28; Acts 20:28)… (4)

---

[60] Rev. C.I. Scofield, The First Reference Bible pg.1258

The Tabernacle a Revelation of Jesus Christ

The N.T. writers ascribe divine perfections and attributes to Christ (e.g. Mt. 11:27; 28:20; 28:20)... (6) N.T. writers teach that supreme worship should be paid to Christ (Acts 7:59,60; 1 For. 1:2)... (7) The holiness and resurrection of Christ prove His deity (Rom. 1:4).[61]

As previously stated the purpose of the table was to "exhibit the bread." Every Sabbath there was the scent of freshly baked bread topped with frankincense filling the Holy Place.

Levy affirms this by commenting:

Twelve New cakes of bread containing about six pounds of flour were arranged into rows of six loaves each. It is not stated in scripture that the bread was unleavened, but it was a meal offering to be used in the tabernacle, it had to be unleavened.[62]

The old loaves were eaten by the priests in the Holy Place, while the frankincense was burned before the

---

[61] Ibid., pg.1144-1145
[62] David M. Levy, Op. cit., pg.52

The Tabernacle a Revelation of Jesus Christ

Lord on the altar of incense. Before the priests could approach the table of showbread which is a type of our communion table, he must understand without reservation, as to how he has arrived at this position, or point on his journey through the tabernacle. One can only get to this point because of the grace of God. The emphasis should never stray from the fact that it is His Mercy, His lovingkindness, and His Faithfulness to us, and He always provides the way for His servants. His grace is always available to all those who seek Him.

Remember we can only see the table which is "before the Lord alway," because of the illuminating light of the lampstand. Without His light of love, grace and mercy we could never stand or partake of that which is upon the table. The table was not for all, nor could it be partaken of in any manner. Just as our communion table has specific guidelines and restrictions; (1 Corinthians 11:23-29). So, the table of showbread could not be approached in any fashion, nor by anyone who pleased. It must be approached according to divine requirements. Let us examine a few of those requirements so we won't be guilty of approaching the Lord's table after the manner of men, but according to the divine pattern.

All ingredients were supplied by the twelve tribes. Slemming offers this truth about the bread:

> The loaves were made of fine flour; nothing coarse or inferior would ever suffice in those things that pointed to the Perfect One. The flour, a product of the earth, had not only to be ground in the mill but sieved, tested, and proved to be "fine" flour before it could be used for showbread, or "presence-bread," or the "bread of faces" as it is sometimes called. This is a picture of the Living Word.[63]

A.B. Simpson offers this thought about the bread: "The bread was unleavened. Not loaves but cakes, because the process of fermentation was the symbol

---

[63] C.W. Slemming, Op. cit., pg.138

of sin and decay. The priests must eat incorruptible bread."[64]

The bread typified Christ the one who knew no sin, but was made sin for us. (2 Corinthians 5:21). He is the righteous one, the Holy one of God. "The bread of God…"

In approaching the table which mirrors our communion (table). We must keep in mind that "The table is not ours, but His. He provided it, He furnishes and orders it, we are only His guests."[65]

J.L. Gonzalez offers this view as to the sacredness of communion in the early church: "…Communion services was that only those who had been baptized could attend…Sometimes converts who had not yet received baptism were allowed in the early part of the service…but were sent away at the time of communion proper."[66]

Here we get an idea of how the early church viewed communion. It was not to be partaken of by anyone

---

[64] A.B. Simpson, Op. cit., pg.66
[65] John Ritchie, Tabernacle in the Wilderness pg.90
[66] Justo L. Gonzalez The Story of the Christian Church Vol. 1 pg94

who is not worthy. The table of showbread was to be revered in the same manner, not all could partake of the bread upon the table, this was exclusively for the priests, who represented the twelve tribes of Israel in the presence of God.

God instructs us on who may approach the table, and how often they were to come. He was very specific in revealing every detail pertaining to its taking. "There shall no stranger eat of the holy thing: a sojourner of the priest, or an hired servant, shall not eat of the holy thing." (Leviticus 22:10). According to J. Ritchie there are three classes of people forbidden to partake of the priest's food. He says:

> They represent three classes of unconverted people. "No stranger." This is one of the descriptions given of man in his natural state (see Eph. 2:11). "No sojourner of the priest." Perhaps an intimate friend come to stay with him for a time, but when the Sabbath day came round he *must* be told that he cannot enter the Holy Place or

eat the holy things…An hired servant shall not eat thereof. A man working for salvation is not to be there…What man soever of the seed of Aaron is a leper, or hath a running issue, he shall not eat the holy things until he be clean…It is no question here of him being a priest. That point was settled, yet by reason of defilement he was for the present disqualified from enjoying the privileges of the priesthood…A true believer may become tainted with leprosy of indulged and cherished evil either doctrinal or moral, so that he becomes unfit to hold communion with a holy God, or to be in fellowship of the saints…Sin is contagious, and if one is permitted to go in and out as he did before, the disease will spread rapidly.[67]

Here we have the solemn sacredness in which God had participants at the table of showbread, and also

---

[67] John Ritchie, Op. cit.,pg.91-92

that the believer today must, "examine himself" before he partakes of the holy communion, otherwise he eats and drinks damnation unto himself. Seeing that the table is the Lord's, He must rule it, and it is His will that must be executed by all those who assemble around it. He provided the table for food to be eaten by the priests on the

Sabbath day in the holy place (Leviticus 24:9).

"We as believer-priests (2 Peter 2:9), are to feed on Christ, the bread of life, receiving in return spiritual sustenance and strength for worship and service. Jesus is the source of our spiritual vitality and fruitfulness in service."[68] Levy certifies this in declaring:

> The bread and wine that sat on the table of showbread spoke of the priests fellowship with the Lord. Our communion with the Lord typifies fellowship as well. On the first day of the week, we gather as a body of believers to have communion with our Lord around the table. We partake of bread and fruit of the vine in remembrance of

---

[68] Davvid M. Levy, Op. cit., pg.55

The Tabernacle a Revelation of Jesus Christ

Jesus' broken body and death on the cross on our behalf (1 Cor. 11:23-26).[69]

Are we as Christians spiritually starving? Are we attending churches that feed us the humanistic, opinions of the world? Are we attending churches that feed us a spiritual experience without sound biblical teaching? We must come to the Lord, so that He can feed us the spiritual bread of God's word, which can edify us for service. "No one has ever come to the table of the Lord to find no food waiting. "[70] Let us all present ourselves before the Table of Showbread as the priests did to partake of the Bread of Life.

---

[69] Loc. Cit.,
[70] C.W. Slemming, Op. cit./, pg.139-140

The Tabernacle a Revelation of Jesus Christ

Chapter 7

The Alter of Incense

And thou shalt make an altar to burn incense upon: of shittim wood shalt thou make it. A cubit shall be the length thereof, and a cubit the breadth thereof; foursquare shall it be: and two cubits shall be the height thereof: the horns thereof shall be of the same. And thou shalt overlay it with pure gold, the top thereof, and the sides thereof round about, and the horns thereof; and thou shalt make unto it a crown of gold round about. And two golden rings shalt thou make to it under the crown of it, by the two corners thereof, upon the two sides of it shalt thou make it; and they shall be for places for the staves to bear it withal. (Exodus 30:1-4).

The golden altar of incense was the third article of furniture in the sanctuary. It was placed directly in front of the veil that separated the Holy Place. It was directly in line with the center of the entrance of the Tabernacle.

The Tabernacle a Revelation of Jesus Christ

The altar of incense was constructed of shittim wood and covered with pure gold. As previously stated this represented the dual natures of Christ, the gold His deity, the wood His humanity. The altar "...which was 36 inches high and 18 inches square was much smaller than the brazen altar."[71] The altar of incense was different from the brazen altar which, was in the outer court before the door. The brazen altar was made of shittim wood and bronze, the altar of incense before the veil was made of shittim wood and gold. The brazen altar was the place of sacrifice, and bloodshed and death. The golden altar was the place of the burning of incense. At each altar , we see Christ revealed. At the brazen altar we see Christ on the cross, who was sacrificed for the sin of the world (John 1:29). His blood was the payment for the penalty of sin, which was death (Romans 6:23). At the altar of incense we see the risen Christ, who makes intercession for us (Hebrews7:25). Christ has become our advocate; He pleads the cause of His redeemed before His father continually.

---

[71] David M. Levy, Op. cit., pg.59

The Tabernacle a Revelation of Jesus Christ

The 17th chapter of John, he gives us a glimpse of the ministry of Christ as an intercessor; " I pray for them: I pray not for the world, but for them which thou hast given me…" (John 17:9). Here we see Christ pleading to His Father on behalf of His disciples for their divine protection. The altar of incense was the place where the priests symbolically offered up prayers on behalf of the entire nation of Israel. Christ also made intercessory prayer not only for His disciples but also for those who would believe on Him "through their word." (John 17:20).

Slemming offers this view:

The altar shows forth the greater work of Christ, who has already accomplished a great work. Having finished the work of redemption from the world, He went up on high to become the great Mediator between God and man, and the great intercessor hearing our cry and pleading our cause. We, as sons of the great High Priest, have received the same high calling in Christ Jesus .[72]

The incense typified: Christ our Intercessor and Mediator. It points to Christ in His ministry of High Priest and Advocate. The incense also typified His name. "Because of the savour of thy good ointments thy name is as ointment poured forth…" (Song of Solomon 1:3). It was also symbolic of prayer. "And when he had taken the book, the four beasts and four and twenty elders fell down before the Lamb, having every one of them harps, and golden vials full of odours, which are the prayers of saints." (Revelation 5:8).

The incense could only be offered by the Aaronic priesthood. This priesthood was a type of the believer-priesthood of today, who have every right as believers to be intercessors, through the much-neglected vehicle of prayer. As believers it is our duty to exercise this ministry daily, and often, for the world needs believers who can petition the Almighty God. When believers intercede God

---

[72] C.W. Slemming, Op. cit., pg.144

answers. He answered Abraham (Genesis 18:23-32), He answered Moses (Exodus 32:31-33), and He will answer us today. Once we sincerely exercise our rights as intercessors. There is no doubt He's looking for intercessors (Ezekiel 22:30).

The purpose of the altar was to burn incense before the Lord. Incense was offered upon the altar daily. It was offered in the morning and in the evening as commanded by God (Exodus 30:708). There could be no deviation from God's prescribed way, for the burning of the incense, nor could there be any deviation from the preparation of the incense to be offered.

Concerning the incense says Levy:

> …Was made from three specific sweet perfumes (Ex. 30:34) mixed with frankincense…" The sweet incense was a beautiful picture of Christ in all His perfections and grace before God and mankind. His life emitted a fragrant perfection of purity and holiness unmarred by sin of fleshly motives. Christians are

The Tabernacle a Revelation of Jesus Christ

called "a sweet savor" to God and the
world (Cor. 2:14-16). As we move through
society, we are like the incense that has
been crushed and burned, emitting the
perfume of the knowledge of Christ to the
glory of God.[73]

All this points to Christ and there could be no
deviations from the divine pattern, the penalty from
such would result in being cut off from the people
of God.

The priests were given the honor, privilege and duty
of ministering at the altar of incense.

Mr. Levy continues:

Before the priests could offer incense of prayer,
three requirements had to be met. First, the priests
had to minister at the brazen altar, shedding the
blood of an animal for their sins. Before we are able
to come before a holy God in prayer, we must be
cleansed by the shed blood of Jesus Christ, which is

---

[73] David M. Levy, Op. cit., pg.60-61

done by appropriating His sacrificial death on the cross on our behalf.

Second, the priests had to wash all defilement from their hands and feet (Ex. 30:18-20) before they could enter the holy place to offer the ministry of prayer. We must confess our sins before God with clean hearts before He will hear our prayers. Third, the priests had to be in the holy place to offer the incense of prayer. Cleansed by the blood and water, they stepped into the sanctuary to fellowship with God...(Heb. 10:22). Aaron was to offer incense on the golden altar at regular times each day (Ex. 30:7-8)...In New Testament times, the disciples kept morning and evening hours of prayer in the temple and their homes (Acts 3:1; 10:9,30), indicating that God desires believers to set aside specific times of prayer throughout the day.[74]

As believers we need to adopt the biblical pattern of prayer. We should offer our prayers, praises and, petitions "without ceasing." We must have a continual attitude of praying all day. We must

---

[74] Ibid., pg.61-62

become intercessors unto God, for the people of God, and for the world. We need to seek God on what methods we can employ to win a dying world for Christ. This can and will become a reality, when we believers revive the fires of intercessory prayer.

There were two stipulations regarding the type of incense and fire that could be used on the altar of incense, Levy suggests:

First, no strange incense could be used on the altar (Ex. 30:9), nor could anyone make the incense of his own personal use (Ex. 30:37). Anyone who did so was "cut off from his people" (put to death) [Ex. 30:38]. This is a figure of prayer offered contrary to God's will. Our prayer life is to conform to the pattern set forth by God in His Word…Our prayers are hindered when we are out of fellowship with God…Second, no fire other than that from the brazen altar could be used on the golden altar…rebellion against the expressed will of God can bring His judgment even on believers…we should not worship and serve God according to the flesh but according to His revealed will in the scriptures.[75]

"And Aaron shall make an atonement upon the horns of it once in a year with the blood of the sin offering of atonements: once in the year shall he make atonement upon it throughout your generations: it is most holy unto the LORD." (Exodus 30:10). The horns of the altar were not just for design, but had a specific purpose. Like the brazen altar it had four horns a "symbol of universal strength & equality."[76] At the altar of incense the horns were overlaid with gold and not bronze as was the brazen altar. The two altars were tied together by the blood sacrifice. On the day of atonement the high priest, according to his assigned duties, would take some of the blood used to sprinkle the mercy seat and "put some of the blood upon the horns of the altar of sweet incense before the LORD…"(Leviticus 4:7). This was done as an act of cleansing, and hollowing the altar from the

---

[75] Ibid., pg.62-63
[76] Shelia Reynolds. Op. cit., pg.46

children of Israel's uncleanness (Leviticus 16:18-19).

C.W. Slemming viewed the horns from this perspective, he says the horns:

...tell the power of prayer, prayer that can reach to the four corners of the earth. Abram interceded for Sodom and prevailed as long as he prayed. Jacob wrestled all night at Peniel and became Israel. Ezekiel pleaded for Jerusalem. We need to lay hold of the horns of prevailing prayer.[77]

The altar of incense is a token of the believers prayer. The value of the altar was not in the wood or the gold but its value was in the incense. The incense that God desires now is that which emanates from the heart.

A.B. Simpson reflects on the ministry of the altar of incense which he says :

> The altar was the highest object in the Tabernacle, several inches higher than the table of shewbread and higher than the

---

[77] C.W. Slemming, Op. cit., pg.143

laver or the brazen altar of sacrifice in the Tabernacle courtyard. So, prayer is the most exalted ministry in the universe. A person on his knees is more elevated than at any other time.[78]

The altar of incense is a type of Christ, our intercessor and mediator. It represents His ministry of high priest and advocate. As believers Christ is our perfect example, we are to be imitators of Christ in every aspect of our lives, let us lay hold to the great ministry of prayer, and remember "a person on his knees is more elevated than at any other time."

---

[78] A.B. Simpson, Op. cit., pg.77

Chapter 8
The Holy Of Holies
The Veil

"And thou shalt make a vail of blue, and purple, and scarlet, and fine twined linen of cunning work: with cherubims shall it be made: And thou shalt hang it upon four pillars of shittim wood overlaid with gold: their hooks shall be of gold, upon the four sockets of silver. And thou shalt hang up the vail under the taches, that thou mayest bring in thither within the vail the ark of the testimony: and the vail shall divide unto you between the holy place and the most holy. And thou shalt put the mercy seat upon the ark of the testimony in the most holy place. And thou shalt set the table without the vail, and the candlestick over against the table on the side of the tabernacle toward the south: and thou shalt put the table on the north side." (Exodus 26:31-35).

Having considered what was on the inside of the Holy Place, the table of showbread, the golden lampstand and the altar of incense, our attention

The Tabernacle a Revelation of Jesus Christ

is now drawn unto the veil. A veil according to Webster's dictionary is: "Any piece of cloth used as a concealing or separating screen or curtain."[79]

Unger's bible dictionary defines the veil as: "The screen separating the Holy Place from the Most Holy Place in the tabernacle and temple."[80]

The veil was a divider or curtain of separation that was used to hide something. The veil was used to conceal the one article of furniture in the Most Holy Place, the Ark of the Covenant. To this room access was barred, even to the high priest. Access was only permitted by the high priest once a year, on the day of atonement with the blood from the burnt sacrifice.

The veil was made "...of blue, and purple, and scarlet, and fine twined linen of cunning work: with cherubims shall it be made..." (Exodus 26:31).

The veil was made much like the inner ceiling of the tabernacle. The fine- lined was a type of the holiness and righteousness of Christ. In the veil there was

---

[79] Simon & Schuster, Webster's New World College Dictionary, pg.1479
[80] Merrill F. Unger, Unger's Bible Dictionary. Pg.1146

The Tabernacle a Revelation of Jesus Christ

three colors, blue, purple and scarlet, it was also inwrought with Cherubim, all pointing to Jesus, the Incarnate one, the only way to God the Father. Although the entrances to the outer court and holy place were made of the same material and colors, they differed from the veil because no Cherubim were woven into their fabric. This was intentional as well as symbolic, cherubim were symbolic of protecting the holiness of God. They were first seen on the east side of the Garden of Eden, "to keep the way of the tree of life." (Genesis 3:24). In the holy place the priests were the only ones to witness the cherubim and they understood the sacredness of God's holiness. The believer-priests today must also understand that God is a Holy God and must be revered as Holy. "And they rest not day and night, saying, Holy, holy, holy, Lord God Almighty, which was, and is, and is to come." (Revelation 4:8). There was always a reminder of the Holiness of God in the Holy Place seen through the inwrought cherubim gazing down from the ceiling of the Holy Place or standing guard at the entrance to the Holy of Holies as they are seen within the veil.

The Tabernacle a Revelation of Jesus Christ

Conner reminds us what the colors represents: "The blue is the color of heaven...purple is a royal color...scarlet is the color of sacrificial blood."[81]

The veil was hung upon four pillars made of shittim wood covered with pure gold (Exodus 26:32), which typify the dual nature of Christ in one person. The four pillars are also symbolic of the four gospel accounts about the life and ministry of Christ, these four pillars are seen upholding the veil which is symbolic of Christ's flesh, or the ministry of Christ after the flesh. As the veil was upheld by four pillars, the four Gospels uphold the revelation of Jesus Christ (2 Corinthians 5:16-17).

The veil served two purposes: first the veil was an entrance whereby the high priest was permitted to enter into the holy of holies once a year on the day of atonement, with the blood from the burnt sacrifice (Hebrews 9:7). Entrance at any other time

---

[81] Kevin J. Conner, Op. cit., pg.67

meant death without delay. Second it was a barrier keeping the priests out, who weren't allowed into the most holy place in the presence of the Most Holy God. The veil testified to every person of the *"middle wall of partition"* (Ephesians 2:14), which separated a Holy God from sinful man. No one could experience atonement except he saw his sinful condition before a Holy God. Conner suggests that: "As long as the veil stands, it speaks an emphatic 'Keep out!'"[82]

The veil was symbolic of the body of Christ. It is only through Christ that we are allowed in the presence of God. "Having therefore, brethren, boldness to enter into the holiest by the blood of Jesus, By a new and living way, which he hath consecrated for us, through the veil, that is to say, his flesh..." (Hebrews 10:19-20). Reynolds sums up this truth in connection with the veil as follows: The inwrought veil-The beauty of this inwrought veil speaks of the incarnation and beauty and perfection of the life of the Lord Jesus Christ. "As

---

[82] Kevin J. Conner, Op. cit., pg.69

86

long as He lived, as long as the veil of His flesh stood, His perfect, sinless life condemns us. As long as He lived there was no full access to the Father."

The dividing wall-The veil standing as a curtain speaks of the great wall of division and separation between God and man as a result of sin. The rent veil-Symbolizes the broken body of the Son of God at calvary (It signified the fulfillment an abolishment of the old covenant and the ushering in the New). The veil had to be rent. Christ had to die. The rent veil points to His rent flesh through which the way to the Father is restored (John 14:16). In the rent veil we behold His body which was broken for us…"[83]

KJ Conner's assessment of the veil is : "that the rent veil ushered in the spiritual realities which had been hidden in the eternal form (Rom. 2:20)…the rent veil speaks to us of the fact that the way into the Holiest of all is now open to men."[84]

---

[83] Shelia Reynolds, Op. cit., pg.48
[84] Kevin J. Conner, Op. cit., pg.69

The Tabernacle a Revelation of Jesus Christ

The Ark of the Covenant

Since we have now gained access into the Holy of Holies, we must take care to enter in with reverence. Inside we will find the Ark of the Covenant, whereupon sits the Mercy Seat (Exodus 25:17-22). Within the ark are found three items: A pot of manna (Exodus 16:11-31,33-34), Aaron's rod (Numbers 17:8-10), and the tables of the law (Exodus 25:21b). The Ark of the Covenant was the first piece of furniture that God instructed Moses to make (Exodus 25:8-12). It was the most magnificent and most hallowed of all the furniture within the tabernacle. The ark was a representation of the throne of God on the earth, It was made of shittim wood covered with pure gold. This spoke of the person of Christ. As previously stated the wood was an incorruptible non-decaying wood which is still common in the Sinai desert region. The gold was symbolic of His deity. According to Conner the items placed within the ark each had a different revelation of the person of the Godhead:

> 1. The tables of the Law...a type of the Father-God, the lawgiver. It was by His

voice that the law was first given. The law is symbolic of all authority and power which is in the hands of the Father.

2. In the Manna we are directed to God the Son who is the bread of life and the Bread of heaven which came down from above (John 6:48-55).

3. Aaron's rod that budded...is a type of God the Holy Spirit, for Aaron's Rod we see the principle of fruitfulness and life (Gal. 5:22-23)....The contents of the ark speaks to us of the "fullness of the Godhead bodily." Everything in the Old Testament finds fulfillment in the Lord Jesus Christ, for "in Him dwelleth all the fullness of the Godhead bodily" (Col.2:9).[85]

The Ark represented the person of God in Christ amongst His redeemed people, the throne of God in the earth, and the Glory of God revealed in Divine order and worship. The Ark was a symbol that God through Christ was in the midst of His people.

---

[85] Kevin J. Conner, Op. cit., pg.27

The Tabernacle a Revelation of Jesus Christ

The Mercy Seat

"And thou shalt make a mercy seat of pure gold: two cubits and a half shall be the length thereof, and a cubit and a half the breadth thereof. And thou shalt make two cherubims of gold, of beaten work shalt thou make them, in the two ends of the mercy seat. And make one cherub on the one end, and the other cherub on the other end: even of the mercy seat shall ye make the cherubims on the two ends thereof. And the cherubims shall stretch forth their wings on high, covering the mercy seat with their wings, and their faces shall look one to another; toward the mercy seat shall the faces of the cherubims be. And thou shalt put the mercy seat above upon the ark; and in the ark thou shalt put the testimony that I shall give thee. And there I will meet with thee, and I will commune with thee from above the mercy seat, from between the two cherubims which are upon the ark of the testimony, of all things which I will give thee in commandment unto the children of Israel." (Exodus 25:17-22).

The Tabernacle a Revelation of Jesus Christ

The Mercy Seat sat on top of the Ark of the Covenant. It was a separate article, which served as a lid rather than a cover. There was no wood in the Mercy Seat, it was made of "pure gold." The Mercy Seat speaks of the throne of the Almighty God. It also represented Christ before He took upon Himself a body of flesh "and dwelt amongst us." The Mercy Seat was the meeting place of God and man (Exodus 25:22).

In the tabernacle there weren't any other seats or chairs other than the Mercy Seat. The reason for this is because the work of the priests was never finished; unlike the priesthood of Christ, "...when he had by himself purged our sins, sat down on the right hand of the Majesty on high..." (Hebrews 1:3). The seat according to Reynolds revealed: "...the mercy God could and would extend toward a sinful people if they came by the prescribed way."[86]

---

[86] Shelia Reynolds. Op. cit., pg.51

The Tabernacle a Revelation of Jesus Christ

On the "two ends" of the Mercy Seat were cherubim or cherubims, the word cherubim is plural for its singular form cherub, and there mounted on each end of the Mercy Seat. The cherubim were made of the same piece of gold as that of the Mercy Seat, forming one solid block of gold. The cherubim with outstretched wings covered the Mercy Seat. According to Epp: "They protected the untainted and absolute holiness of God as He is seen to be in the Mercy Seat dwelling among His sinful people."[87]

The purpose of the Mercy Seat was for propitiation, which represented Christ who is our "...propitiation through faith in His blood..." (Romans 3:25). Both Conner and Epp agree that: "The Greek word used here for propitiation is the same Greek word used in Hebrews 9:5 which is translated "Mercy-Seat."[88] Epp states that: "...by comparing Romans 3:26 and Hebrews 9:5 we see that Jesus Christ fulfilled that to which the Mercy Seat pointed."[89] Christ is the

---

[87] Theodore H. Epp, Op. cit., pg.137
[88] Kevin J. Conner, Op. cit., pg.24
[89] Theodore H. Epp, Op. cit., pg.138

satisfaction for our sins! The Mercy Seat typified Him because He "…is the propitiation for our sins: and not only for ours only, but also for the sins of the whole world." (John 2:2).

Within the Most Holy Place on the seat of pure gold, under the extended wings of the cherubim, we see the blood. This was the most sacred place of all. On the Day of Atonement, the high priest carried the blood of the burnt offering into the holy of holies and sprinkled the Mercy Seat to make atonement for the sins of the entire nation. According to Simpson: "It constantly remained there, pleading for the people, standing as a type of Christ's precious life."[90] Here is the place where we have longed to be, the place where God is, the place of special worship. There is no other place a believer should ever strive to be except where the presence of God is. In the camp of Israel, He chose the Blood-stained Mercy Seat, today it's the Blood washed believer. "For the life of the flesh is in the blood: and I have given it to you upon the altar to make an atonement

---

[90] A.B. Simpson, Op. cit., pg.32

The Tabernacle a Revelation of Jesus Christ

for your souls: for it is the blood that maketh an atonement for the soul." (Leviticus 17:11).

BIBLIOGRAPHY

Conner, Kevin j., <u>The Tabernacle of Moses</u>,
Portland, Oregon: Bible Temple Publishing, 1976.

Epp, Theodore H., <u>Portraits of Christ in the
Tabernacle,</u>
Lincoln, Nebraska: Back to the Bible Publication

Gonzalez, L. Justo., <u>The Story of Christianity
Volume 1 The Early Church to the Dawn of the
Reformation,</u>
New York, NY: Harper Collins Publishers, 1984

Habershon, Ada R., <u>Outline Studies of the
Tabernacle</u> Grand Rapids, Michigan: Kregel
Publications, 1974

Levy, David, M., <u>The Tabernacle Shadows of the
Messiah Its Sacrifices, Services, and Priesthood,</u>
Belwar, NJ: The Friends of Israel Gospel Ministry,
Inc. 1993

The Tabernacle a Revelation of Jesus Christ

Reynolds, Shelia. Lecture. "The Tabernacle". Brooklyn, NY Unpublished.

Ritchie, John., Tabernacle in the Wilderness, Grand Rapids, Michigan: Kregel Publications, 1982.

Scofield, C.I. Rev., The First Scofield Reference Bible, Iowa Falls: World Bible Publishers, 1986.

Simpson, A.B., Christ in the Tabernacle, Camphill, PA: Christian Publications, 1985

Simon & Schuster, Inc., Webster's New World College Dictionary, MacMillian General Reference New York, NY 1996

Slemming, C.W., Made According to the Pattern, Fort Washington, PA: Christian Literature Crusade (Revised edition), 1999.

The Tabernacle a Revelation of Jesus Christ

Soltau, Henry, W., The Tabernacle the Priesthood and Offerings, Grand Rapids, Michigan: Kregel Publications, 1994

Strong, James., The New Strong's Exhaustive Concordance of the Bible, Nashville, Tennessee: Thomas Nelson Publishers, 1990.

Under, Merrill F., Unger's Bible Dictionary, Chicago Illinois: Moody Press., 1966.

The Tabernacle a Revelation of Jesus Christ

www.ingramcontent.com/pod-product-compliance
Lightning Source LLC
Chambersburg PA
CBHW052156090426
42741CB00010B/2293